Seeds of Blessings

Michael Amamieye

Unless otherwise stated, all scripture quotations are from the King James Version of the Bible.

All rights reserved.

Copyright©2001, Michael O. Amamieye
Reprinted 2020

Published by:

**Michael Amamieye Word Outreach, International
also known as
Aggressive Faith Ministries,
Plot 13 Walter Akpana Lay Out off 394 Ikwerre Road
Mile 5 Rumueprikom
P. O. Box 12378, Port Harcourt, Nigeria.
Phone: +2349018006296, +2348050987377,
WhatsApp: +2348036732188
U.S.A.: +19162456157
Website: www.aggressivefaith.org
Email: info@aggressivefaith.org**

ISBN: 978–978-51071-1-1

PRINTED IN THE FEDERAL REPUBLIC OF NIGERIA

WARNING

I did not write this book. I was inspired. The Spirit of prophecy did.

As you read, the Spirit of prophecy will come over you, overshadow you and a seed shall be formed in you. That seed is the Seed of Blessing.

You shall be transformed and you shall have testimonies to the glory of God in Jesus name. Amen.

Table of Content

Dedication

*I want to dedicate this book to three women who changed
my life:
First to my dear grandmother, Madam Betty Kopre,
Second, to my dear mother, Madam Maria Ebikefe
And to my dear wife, Princess Monivi.*

INTRODUCTION

God is the God of blessing. How do I know that? Looking at the Bible which is God's word from Genesis to Revelation, I see God blessing His creation especially man. Before man, everything God created, He blessed. He is so full of the blessing that everything gets a dosage of the blessing. You will discover later in this book that the blessing also means to speak well of. You can see that God was speaking well of everything He created when He said, *"…it was good…"* Gen. 1:4. This happened every day after He created something.

Eventually when He created, He finished creation by saying, *"…behold, it was very good…"* Gen. 1:31. He spoke well of everything He created. No wonder everything God created looked really good because His words painted them good.

After He created man, He blessed him. This blessing was very important for man to be like God on earth. It was important for man to be able to exercise dominion on earth. It was important for man to be able to exercise authority over Satan and all fallen angels we now know as demons. This blessing was what forces man to be fruitful, multiply, replenish the earth, subdue it and have dominion.

"And God blessed them, and God said unto them, Be fruitful, and multiply, and replenish the earth, and subdue it: and have dominion over the fish of the sea, and over the fowl of the air, and over every living thing that moveth upon the earth."
Gen. 1:28.

Can you imagine for a second, if the first man needed the blessing in that world where there was not the kind of wickedness and evil we have to deal with today, how much more you and me? I have come to conclude that I need the blessing of God to survive the evil of this world. I need the blessing of God to overcome the evil one. I need the blessing of God to overcome sin, sickness, sorrow, suffering and shame. I need the blessing of God to overcome Satan and his angels. I know that you too need the blessing of God. That is why I have written this book to unleash the blessing of God in your life.

The first thing God did to man when He created man was to bless man. He knows that man needs the blessing to live here on earth. Interestingly, the last thing Jesus did before He ascended to heaven was to release the blessing on His disciples.

"And he led them out as far as to Bethany, and he lifted up his hands, and blessed them.

And it came to pass, while he blessed them, he was parted from them, and carried up into heaven.
And they worshipped him, and returned to Jerusalem with great joy:
And were continually in the temple, praising and blessing God. Amen."
Luke 24:50-53.

Think about it for a second: the last thing Jesus did was to bless His disciples. As He blessed them, He was taken up to heaven. The blessing transformed them. They were not afraid or speechless. They worshipped and returned to Jerusalem with great joy. That is what the blessing can do for you. The blessing creates great joy even in the midst of great crisis. This is one major reason man needs the blessing to change chaotic situations to moments of great joy. You can never be miserable with the blessing. The blessing has the capacity to turn trying times to triumphant times.

In Gen. 1:2, we see the actual state of the earth before man was created. It was without form. It was void and unproductive. Nothing good could come out of it. It was dark as darkness took over every space.

"And the earth was without form, and void; and darkness was upon the face of the deep. And the Spirit of God moved upon the face of the waters."
Gen. 1:2.

It was in the midst of this chaos as it were man was created and positioned to change everything. Man could not do it without the blessing. I see why this book is relevant for this moment. You can read the news or see around you the damaging impact of the pandemic. The economy of practically every nation on earth has been adversely impacted. Some countries are already in recession right now. However, God has allowed us to be here at a time like this. We are the ones He is counting on to change the situation from hopelessness to hopefulness. How can we do that? The blessing is what we need.

This book is in your hand today because I believe that God wants you to be part of the transformation of our world at this times with the blessing mandate that you will receive as you read through, meditate on and express the blessing of God in your corner. Get ready to be part of the new world changer by the blessing.

1

DEFINITION OF TERMS

*S*ocrates, the father of philosophy, said that if two intelligent people must communicate intelligently, they must first define their terms. This is so important because this word **blessing** is one word that has been abused in recent times.

Among Christians, you find some greet, *bless you*. For them, blessing is a greeting. I want to submit to you that to greet an elder that way is total disrespect. Actually, it takes an elder or better person to bless a younger or lesser person.

> *"and as everyone knows, a person who has the power to bless is always greater than the person he blesses."*
> Heb 7:7. The Living Bible.

Only a bigger, better, greater, richer person can greet you, Bless you, and it can make a huge difference in your life. So the next time someone better than you tells you, Bless you, you will receive it with understanding that can literally change your condition. The hard truth is that a beggar cannot bless a giver. Only a giver can bless a beggar. However, bless you, goes beyond greetings. It is power untapped. It is power that can totally change the dynamics of events and happenings around you.

For some, when someone sneezes they say, bless you. Now, I wonder if they are blessing the person with more sneezes. Don't bless me with more sneezes because I don't need it. Instead of blessing them with more sneezes, you can say to them, IT IS WELL WITH YOU!

"Say ye to the righteous, that it shall be well with him: for they shall eat the fruit of their doings."
Isa. 3:10.

Thank God for the pandemic that has changed the impact of sneezing. People are scared to sneeze in public places now because the center for disease control can be alerted that they have the corona virus. But let me help you right there. Even if you sneeze, speak God's word to your body, IT IS WELL WITH ME IN JESUS NAME. That alone can cure the virus. Keep on speaking it until the virus leaves and it will leave at God's word. No sickness or disease or virus can survive the power of God's word.

There are some who use the word blessing to close a letter or communication. I still don't understand what that means even though I do it sometimes. If I don't get the blessing before the conversation closes why close it with a blessing? That is a misnomer. It is proper to have an understanding of the word we use to make sense.

In defining the terminologies used for blessing, I will take you on a journey through both Hebrew and Greek words. This is because these words are very rich and deep in both languages. As you know, the English word sometimes is very limited. So when you try to translate a word from your native language if you are not English by native, you lose so much force. Words when spoken in our native languages most times carry a heavier weight. As you go through this book, you will receive light that will brighten your life.

BLESS

The Hebrew word for bless is *barak.* It means to *kneel down* as an act of adoration, worship, fervent and devoted love. It also means to benefit or to bestow a divine influence on.

The Psalmist David said, *"I will bless the LORD, who hath given me counsel…"* Psa. 16:7. The implication of this is that David meant to kneel before God in adoration and worship for what God bestowed on him. The Lord gave him *counsel* which gave him a divine influence to overcome his enemies. For that reason, as a show of his fervent and devoted love to God, he knelt down to adore and worship God.

This presupposes that before we can receive from God we need to kneel down in adoration and worship. Before the ministry of the word, teach the people to kneel before God in adoration and worship. After the ministry of the word, teach them to kneel in adoration and worship to God. Your attitude can determine your reception. That is why it is said that the hand of the giver is always on top of the hand of the receiver. It is an attitude that makes one a giver and a receiver.

Before Jesus fed the multitude, He told them to sit down. *"And he commanded the multitude to sit down on the grass…"* Matt 14:19. The phrase *'sit down'* means to *fall down*. It means to reduce your height. The Canaanite woman did not get Jesus' attention until she came, *"…and worshipped him…"* Matt. 15:25. Humility is proper position for honor. *"…before honour is humility."* Prov. 15:33.

The Greek word for bless is *eulogeo*. It means to *speak well of*, to praise, to prosper. It also means to invoke good things upon. When you bless God or man, it means that you are speaking well of them. You are emphasizing those good aspects of their lives that have touched you or someone else. You praise God or man when you bless them.

You can now see how to bless your spouse or partner or children or parents or employer or employee by speaking well of them. Every time you speak badly of someone, you are not blessing them, you will be doing the exact opposite. Oh Lord, help me to always bless my wife, my children, my staff, my team members, my partners, my pastor, etc. Let us make a huge difference in people's lives by speaking well of them. Emphasize the good sides of your neighbor or colleague or relation and you will see the difference.

That is how we bless God by speaking well of Him. Some people may really not understand how you can speak well of God when they are hungry or sick or broke or suffer some loss. However, as you speak well of Him of the things He has done that may be little, you will change the situation that looks so bad because your God will become bigger.

To bless also means to prosper. It means to speak the things that will cause them to prosper. Nobody can prosper if you keep telling him or her that they cannot make it. As a father, whenever you tell your child that he or she can make it, you are blessing that child. Every good invocation or pronouncement you make over your life is a blessing. Parents, stop speaking badly of your children. You think that you are telling the truth about them. No, you are actually removing every possibility for them to become better. As a spouse, speak well of your partner. Stop badmouthing them before your friends or colleagues or neighbors thinking you are just joking or telling it like it is. Your speaking empowers or demobilizes.

Another word for bless is the word benefit or benefits. The Hebrew *yatab* means to make better, to amend, to be well, to make well, sound, beautiful, happy, successful and right. You bless someone with your words or works or wealth by making them better, beautiful, happy, successful and right. You know that you have been a blessing because they are better than you met them. When you meet people, leave them better. Don't leave them miserable or feeling like losers.

God told Abraham, ***"...I will bless thee..."*** Gen 12:2. By implication, God meant He was going to make Abraham's life better. Indeed, Abraham became better, bigger, richer and greater. Abraham turned out to be very influential and successful. When God blesses you, He makes your life better. You cannot be blessed by God and still be bitter in life. You will be better for life. God's blessing will make you well, sound, beautiful, happy and successful.

BLESSED

The Hebrew word for blessed is ***asher***. It means to be straight, to make right, to be happy. That implies that if God blesses you, you will walk straight, you will be straight. No gay or homosexual or lesbian is blessed. You can't be blessed by God and be gay. Even if you were crooked before you encountered the blessing of God, it will straighten you. It also means to go forward and to prosper.

Crooked people are not blessed. We have seen people in power or positions of power or possession who are not blessed. You can use crooked means to acquire things yet you are not blessed. A blessed man is different. A blessed man changes the atmosphere. When a blessed man is in authority, he will make right what is wrong. The people will be happy. Blessed people make people happy. That is why any government that is making the people miserable is not blessed by God.

*"When the righteous are in authority, the people rejoice:
but when the wicked beareth rule, the people mourn."*
Prov. 29:2.

A blessed man is empowered to go forward and to prosper. When you say that someone is blessed it means that they are empowered to prosper. It is the ability, authority and audacity to prosper. Give two people the same opportunity or opening, the one who is blessed makes something out of what looks like nothing to the other. The blessing definitely makes a huge difference.

"And God said, Let us make man in our image, after our likeness: and let them have dominion over the fish of the sea, and over the fowl of the air, and over the cattle, and

over all the earth, and over every creeping thing that creepeth upon the earth.
So God created man in his own image, in the image of God created he him; male and female created he them.
And God blessed them, and God said unto them, Be fruitful, and multiply, and replenish the earth, and subdue it: and have dominion over the fish of the sea, and over the fowl of the air, and over every living thing that moveth upon the earth."
Gen 1: 26-28.

Man was created in the image and likeness of God. But he could not act like God until he was empowered. When God blessed them, He literally empowered them to be fruitful, multiply, replenish the earth, subdue it and have dominion. God literally gave them the ability, authority and audacity to be fruitful, multiply, replenishes the earth, subdue it and have dominion. By that, no matter how unproductive the earth was, this man can turn it around. The location does not determine the production. It is the person that determines the product.

BLESSING

The Hebrew word for blessing or blessings is the word **berakah**. It simply means prosperity, present, liberal or benediction. Every time we share the benediction, we are supposed to prophesy or utter the blessing to embolden us to face the challenges ahead. It is meant to energize and empower us for what is ahead. The blessing makes you liberal not locked up. The blessing frees you to prosper. It does not restrain you. it removes all the barriers and barricades that stops others.

Let us consider the word prosperity. There are four Hebrew words that will help us here. The Hebrew *towb* means to be, to do, to make good, well, better, beautiful. It means to be well favored. It also means welfare, wealth, sweet. The blessing makes you to become well, better and beautiful. The blessing makes you to do good. The blessing is a maker. It makes. You see why I love the blessing. It makes you beautiful. You can be ugly physically but the blessing transforms you to become so beautiful. The blessing makes you well and wealthy. Don't blame me when you see me well and wealthy. I am not to blame. Blame the blessing. Instead of getting jealous or envious, covet the blessing. It will definitely make the difference in your life.

"The blessing of the LORD, it maketh rich, and he addeth no sorrow with it."
Prov. 10:22.

The Hebrew *shalowm* means to be safe, well, happy and friendly. The blessing makes you safe, sound, well, happy and friendly. It makes you friendly. A blessed man has many friends. Now you understand why some people complain that they don't have friends. The fact is that they are not yet blessed. If by this they covet the blessing, in no distant time, they will testify of how the blessing has transformed them. The blessing makes you friendly and attracts friends to you.

"The poor is hated even of his own neighbour: but the rich hath many friends."
Prov 14:20.

The Hebrew *tsalach* means to push forward, to break out, to go over, to be profitable. The blessing of the Lord makes you push forward. That desire to push forward, breakthrough and make profit is a blessing from the Lord. Each time you make progress and profit is a blessing from the Lord. The blessing of God empowers you to push forward where others quit or are afraid to step out. The blessing pushes you to break out of moulds and boxes the society or system or someone set for you. they may have told you that you can't do this or that. The blessing will empower you to do what they said you can't.

"The sons of the prophets said to Elisha, Look now, the place where we live before you is too small for us."
2 Kings 6:1. (Amplified Version).

It was the blessing that made those boys make that statement. They wanted more. Each time you ask for more, it is a sign of the blessing making you. The blessing makes you want more. This is why when your child asks for more, don't shut them down. It is a blessing. When your spouse asks for more, don't quarrel with them. It is a blessing. When your employer or employee ask for more, don't strike or clam down on them. It is a blessing. The blessing will expand your space. You will become uncomfortable with smallness and mediocrity. You will become dissatisfied with peanuts and paltry wages. The blessing gives you the audacity to ask for more than what they think you deserve.

The Hebrew **shalev** means to be secure or successful. It also means to be happy, to be in safety, to be tranquil, to be careless and to be peaceable. The blessing of the Lord makes you happy, safe, secured and careless. It takes sorrow, worry and anxiety out of your life. The blessing can make you care less about what people say. People will always say what they think about you. The blessing will surprise them for you. There will be questions people will ask that you can't answer. Only the blessing can answer them.

Another word for blessing is the word liberal. The Hebrew **nadiyb** means to offer freely, willingly. It also means to volunteer and to be generous. The Greek **haplotes** means copious in giving. It means giving in abundance. Only the blessing can make a man or woman so liberal that they give themselves, their time, their talent and treasures for a cause that others don't think is profitable. A blessed man will make it look profitable. The blessing makes people willing to give generously. In my work as an evangelist for well over three decades, I have seen that it is not rich people who give to the gospel. Instead, it is blessed people who give.

In fact, I like the Hebrew *anaq* translated liberally. It means to choke with supplies, to strangle with abundance, to furnish. This is the place where God wants us to get to. If someone asks you for one dollar, you give ten. You literally choke them with abundance. Husbands, when your wife ask you for a hundred dollar, choke her with one thousand dollar. You will see the difference it makes in your relationships. I remember one of my cousins who is older than me greet me in our traditional way where a younger person greets an elder. I had to remind him that he is not supposed to do that. He did it because he was choked with the blessing of God on my life.

"But now I tell you: do not take revenge on someone who wrongs you. If anyone slaps you on the right cheek, let him slap your left cheek too.
And if someone takes you to court to sue you for your shirt, let him have your coat as well.
And if one of the occupation troops forces you to carry his pack one mile, carry it two miles.

When someone asks you for something, give it to him; when someone wants to borrow something, lend it to him."
Matt. 5:39–42. (Today's English Version)

The Greek word for blessing or blessings is ***eulogia***. It means fine speaking, commendation, adoration, benediction, benefit, largess. I really love this. Fine speaking. When you are blessed, you speak fine. You don't curse or swear like those people who are not blessed. Have you noticed that blessed people are relaxed? They are not as ruffled or edgy as others. I like that.

The word commendation, Greek ***sustatikos***, means to strengthen, to make to stand, to exhibit, to introduce. The blessing strengthens, emboldens and empowers you. It makes you to stand where others fall. It exhibits or manifests you. It introduces you. When you become a blessing, you become a strengthener for others. You become the one who makes others stand. You manifest them. You literally introduce them. A blessed man will be liberal to exhibit and introduce others. He is not afraid that they might pluck mango from where they pluck their oranges. A blessed man is not intimidated by others.

Moses introduced Joshua. Elijah introduced Elisha. John the Baptist introduced Jesus. Who have you introduced to that trade, business, ministry, etc? For you to be a blessing you need introduction. Let Jehovah God introduce you. That is a blessing

The blessing makes you good at imparting. It makes you ready to distribute.

"Tell those who are rich in this world not to be proud and not to trust in their money, which will soon be gone. But their trust should be in the living God, who richly gives us all we need for our enjoyment.
Tell them to use their money to do good. They should be rich in good works and should give generously to those in need, always being ready to share with others whatever God has given them.
By doing this they will be storing up their treasure as a good foundation for the future so that they may take hold of real life."
1 Tim. 6: 17-19. (New Living Translation)

2

INSTRUMENTS OF BLESSING

*I*n legal parlance, there is what is called the power of attorney. It is the power or right to something. It is a written document that empowers a person or party to act in the stead of someone.

This is exactly what the blessing does to us. It empowers us to act as blessed people of God. Some of us came from cursed heathen backgrounds. But the blessing empowers us to act contrary to where we are coming from. The reason why we can act the blessing is because we have been copiously blessed to the point that the blessing is flowing out of us. It is a way to live not a stage act.

To ensure ceaseless flow of the blessing into our lives and the lives of others through us, there are three instruments I want to show you. Blessings are passed on from God to us and through us through these three instruments: ***words***, ***works*** and ***wealth.***

WORDS

The most powerful instrument of life is words. They carry the very power of divinity. For **Elohim**, the possessor of power, might and ability chose to encode Himself in **The Word** is a mystery. Think of it, God is **The Word**. He did not choose any other instrument but **The Word.**

"In the beginning was the Word, and the Word was with God, and the Word was God."
John 1:1.

To show you how powerful **The Word** is, He (Jehovah God) magnified it above all His names. As powerful as His names are, His word is more powerful than His names. His word is what literally gives His names the power they have. That is why He magnifies, makes bigger, larger, His word above His names.

"I will worship toward thy holy temple, and praise thy name for thy lovingkindness and for thy truth: for thou hast magnified thy word above all thy name."
Psa. 138:2.

The power of *The Word* is seen in creation as everything created, visible and invisible, are products of *The Word.*

"All things were made by him; and without him was not any thing made that was made."
John 1:3.

"By faith we understand that the worlds [during the successive ages] were framed (fashioned, put in order, and equipped for their intended purpose) by the word of God, so that what we see was not made out of things which are visible."
Heb. 11:3. Amplified Version.

All created beings and things are sustained by *The Word.*

"He is the sole expression of the glory of God [the Light-being, the out-raying or radiance of the divine], and He is the perfect imprint and very image of [God's] nature, upholding and maintaining and guiding and propelling the universe by His mighty word of power. When He had by offering Himself accomplished our cleansing of sins and riddance of guilt, He sat down at the right hand of the divine Majesty on high."
Heb. 1:3. Amplified Version.

Words are vehicles. They travel very far. Eccl. 10:20 tells us that words have wings. The word spoken in your bedchambers can be heard on the housetop. What you know today are pieces of information put to words and handed down to you from generations passed.

Words are containers and carriers. They carry the forces that make for life and death. People have died because of words spoken carelessly. I remember hearing a comedian tell a tragic joke about a man who went to his neighbor to apologize for using his Wi-Fi while he was gone to work. What this neighbor heard was wife instead of Wi-Fi. Well, his confession turned to his death sentence. People live or die because of words. Wars have been caused by words. Chaos is caused by words. Disagreements are caused by words. Community crisis are caused by words. Divorce in marriage have been caused by words.

"Words kill, words give life; they're either poison or fruit —
you choose."
Prov. 18:21. THE MESSAGE.

Words carry healing and health. People have become sick because of words. I watched a comedy skit on Facebook recently where a woman fell asleep. When she woke up, someone had used ketchup with plaster to create a fake surgical mark on her stomach. As she was waking up, the person told her that she just came out of surgery. She touched the spot and immediately she began to feel the pain. She took her phone to call her dad. As she was telling him, she carefully tried to open up the wound to see only to discover it was fake. It was fake yet she felt the pain when she heard that she just came out of surgery. People have also been healed because someone told them nothing was wrong with them.

"Dear friend, listen well to my words; tune your ears to my voice.
Keep my message in plain view at all times. Concentrate! Learn it by heart!
Those who discover these words live, really live; body and soul, they're bursting with health."
Prov. 4:20-22. THE MESSAGE.

"Some people like to make cutting remarks, but the words of the wise soothe and heal."
Prov. 12:18. The Living Bible.

Words carry deliverance. People get delivered by words. People will be delivered by words. Deliverance is the result of words well directed. People have been delivered from death because they heard and heeded the right words. There are people who have been delivered from natural disasters because they heard and heeded the right words.

"The words of the wicked are, "Lie in wait for blood," But the mouth of the upright will deliver them."
Prov. 12:6. New King James Version

Words carry food for many. People are hungry because they have not heard the right words that show them where there is food. During the lockdown, most people were hungry. Some even died of hunger because of what they heard. Words can determine whether you will have food or not.

"The lips of the righteous feed many: but fools die for want of wisdom."
Prov. 10:21.

Words carry the forces and fruits that bring satisfaction. There are wives who are happy with their husbands because the men know how to use the right words to make the women happy. There are husbands who are crazy about their wives because the women know the right words to make the men happy. There are employees who will die for their employers because the employers use the right words on them. If you want to see certain results as fruits, you have to sow the seed that produces the fruits. If you want your marriage to be happy, sow happy seeds. Sow the right words to your spouse and enjoy the fruits of your seeds.

"A man shall be satisfied with good by the fruit of his mouth: and the recompence of a man's hands shall be rendered unto him."
Prov. 12:14.

"A man shall eat good by the fruit of his mouth: but the soul of the transgressors shall eat violence."
Prov. 13:2

There is a spiritual law I call the law of sustenance. It states that everything is sustained by its source. Fish came out of water. It can only be sustained in a water environment. If you take fish out of water to a land environment, in no distant time it will die. No matter how golden or gorgeous the environment is, if it is not a water environment that fish will die.

Everything was created by the word of God including man. All of God's creation can only be sustained by His word. This is the reason God's creation answer to His word. You can speak God's word to the sun and moon like Joshua did and they will obey you because they can hear God's word in your voice. You may think that they are obeying you. Actually, it is God they are obeying because you spoke His word.

*"Then spake Joshua to the Lord in the day when the Lord delivered up the Amorites before the children of Israel, and he said in the sight of Israel, Sun, stand thou still upon Gibeon; and thou, Moon, in the valley of Ajalon.
And the sun stood still, and the moon stayed, until the people had avenged themselves upon their enemies. Is not this written in the book of Jasher? So the sun stood still in the midst of heaven, and hasted not to go down about a whole day."*
Jos. 10:12,13.

Prophetess Deborah spoke God's word and the stars obeyed.

"They fought from heaven; the stars in their courses fought against Sisera."
Judges 5:20.

The sun, moon, stars and the entire hosts of heaven have been assigned to all of us. We are not to worship them. We are to use them to battle our enemies like Joshua and Deborah did.

"And lest thou lift up thine eyes unto heaven, and when thou seest the sun, and the moon, and the stars, even all the host of heaven, shouldest be driven to worship them, and

serve them, which the Lord thy God hath divided unto all nations under the whole heaven."
Deut. 4:19.

Jesus spoke to the sea to be still and it obeyed.

"And he arose, and rebuked the wind, and said unto the sea, Peace, be still. And the wind ceased, and there was a great calm."
Mark 4:39.

He has said that if we speak to a tree to be rooted out of the earth and planted in the sea. He said that the tree, *"...should obey you."* Luke 17:6. It will be surprising if that tree disobeys you.

The implication of that statement of truth is that everything around your life and in your life responds to the words of your mouth. Your body is controlled by the words of your mouth. Your words can defile your body or make it clean. The words of your mouth determine the course of events and happenings around your life.

"And the tongue is a fire. [The tongue is] a world of wickedness set among our members, contaminating and depraving the whole body and setting on fire the wheel of

birth (the cycle of man's nature), being itself ignited by hell (Gehenna)."
James 3:6 (Amplified Version)

Do you love to live a good life? Then keep your tongue from evil. 1 Pet. 3:9-11. Psa. 34:12-14.

Enrich your life with good words. The problem here is that you cannot do it if your heart is filled with evil. You must consciously, deliberately and decisively take out all the evil thoughts, words and deeds in your heart. Throw them out by nailing them to the cross of Calvary. Then, store God's word in your heart. Treasure good thoughts, words and deed in your heart until it overflows. Out of the overflow you will become accustomed to speaking good things. Matt. 7:16-20. 12:23-37. Mark 7:14-23. Luke 6:43-45.

Words that flow towards us in our thoughts, through association and interaction, through what we hear, see and read will either bless or curse us. They carry the vital forces of life and death, blessing and cursing, good and evil.

When God blessed man, He spoke words of fruitfulness, multiplication, etc. ***"And God blessed them, and God said unto them…"*** Gen. 1:28. When He commanded the priests to bless His people, He told the priests to speak the blessing into the lives of the people. ***"…On this wise ye shall bless the children of Israel, saying unto them."*** Num. 6:23. The blessing is released by words.

WORKS

The next most powerful instrument of life is what we call works. Works are those things you do daily. They are the things that occupy you. It can be seen as your occupation.

> *"And he called his ten servants, and delivered them ten pounds, and said unto them, Occupy till I come."*
> Luke 19:13.

The word, ***occupy***, comes from the word pragmatic, Greek, ***pragmateuomai.*** It simply means to be practical, to busy yourself with, to trade. Works are the practical aspects of words. The blessing released in words should be translated to works. You have to work it out. The word works when you work it.

If you have confessed that Jesus is Lord of your life, don't let it end with your words. Work those words by manifesting a lifestyle that is submissive to Him. If you have received the word of healing, don't lie on that sick bed. Work the word out by an act of being healed. Don't act like you are still sick so that people will pity you. Act the healing and health that you have received.

Your attitude and acts must correspond with the words of blessing you have received. Did you receive a word of blessing of the fruit of the womb? Then, carry yourself like a pregnant woman marking time to deliver. Pregnant women know how to mark time because they are taught so during antenatal clinic sessions. This is good for you because it gives you hope. It makes you expectant. Every pregnant woman is an expectant mother. They look forward to the delivery day.

Works are the results of calling. A calling is an invitation, an appointment, a vocation, an opportunity, a duty, and an assignment. Each time you are given an invitation to accept Christ or an assignment is a calling. Your response to it is your work. If you are given an opportunity to serve, that is a calling. Your response to it is your work.

Works have three elements: season, time and purpose.

"To every thing there is a season, and a time to every purpose under the heaven:
I know that, whatsoever God doeth, it shall be for ever: nothing can be put to it, nor any thing taken from it: and God doeth it, that men should fear before him."
Eccl. 3:1,14.

Season, Hebrew, *zeman*, are those occasions, appointments and opportunities that come to us not regularly. They don't come to us daily. They are occasioned by need, seed or deed. When these occasions or opportunities or appointments come, your response is your works. What you do about them can determine your future for life. Many of us have missed such occasion that is why we are not blessed.

"Cast thy bread upon the waters: for thou shalt find it after many days.
Give a portion to seven, and also to eight; for thou knowest not what evil shall be upon the earth.
If the clouds be full of rain, they empty themselves upon the earth: and if the tree fall toward the south, or toward the north, in the place where the tree falleth, there it shall be.
He that observeth the wind shall not sow; and he that regardeth the clouds shall not reap.
As thou knowest not what is the way of the spirit, nor how the bones do grow in the womb of her that is with child: even so thou knowest not the works of God who maketh all.
In the morning sow thy seed, and in the evening withhold not thine hand: for thou knowest not whether shall prosper, either this or that, or whether they both shall be alike good."
Eccl. 11:1-6.

If there is any regret I have today, it is those seasons to plant my best seed that I missed. Those seasons to take up a responsibility that was put on me and I excused myself. O

God, restore unto me those wasted seasons and opportunities. When God called me to world evangelism in 1984, I tried to travel for six years to Cotonou, Benin Republic. For whatever reason, I just could not. I will plan and just never saw my plans materialized. One day, I saw an advert about the Billy Graham conference for evangelists in Amsterdam. I took advantage of it and that one door opened up the world to me. Today, I have taken the gospel of Christ to seventy two nations. One of my friends I gave the same invitation to played with it until I left for the conference. Till today, he is still struggling in ministry trying to find his place. One missed opportunity can determine a life time of struggles.

Seasons come as those opportunities to meet a need which can determine your next life in life. I will never forget when I attended a conference in Cotonou, Benin Republic some years ago. I needed a place to stay. I stumbled on a man of God who had a hotel room he lodged. He took me in and we had a good time at that conference. He met my need for accommodation. As it turned out, I invited him to Nigeria. Initially, he did not believe me when I told him that I will put him on television to minister the gospel and open up doors for him to preach the gospel. Actually, he did not believe me. So, instead of coming to me, he visited another friend of mine. His expectations were almost cut short. Towards the end of his stay with my friend, he remembered me and decided to contact me. I put him in a hotel for the rest of his stay with us. He was on television and radio. He ministered in several churches. He was so blessed with a lot of gifts. To cap it up, I took him to a meeting where he met with the international director of a global organization. He became the Ghana Director of that organization. That opened up the door for him to the United States of America and other parts.

Your season can change when you are sensitive to meet some needs or plant some seeds or do something that you don't normally do.

Another important element of works is timing. There is time for everything under the sun.

"To every thing there is a season, and a time to every purpose under the heaven:
A time to be born, and a time to die; a time to plant, and a time to pluck up that which is planted;
A time to kill, and a time to heal; a time to break down, and a time to build up;
A time to weep, and a time to laugh; a time to mourn, and a time to dance;
A time to cast away stones, and a time to gather stones together; a time to embrace, and a time to refrain from embracing;
A time to get, and a time to lose; a time to keep, and a time to cast away;

A time to rend, and a time to sew; a time to keep silence, and a time to speak;
A time to love, and a time to hate; a time of war, and a time of peace."
Eccl. 3:1–8.

The beauty of any work is the timing. If you do a good work at the wrong time, it can be messy. But when it is the right time, it is beautiful.

"He hath made every thing beautiful in his time: also he hath set the world in their heart, so that no man can find out the work that God maketh from the beginning to the end."
Eccl. 3:11.

In the Bible, you will find several qualifications for time. There is the **appointed time** which is fixed before the foundation of the world by God. Only God knows this time and to whomsoever He chooses to reveal it.

"Is there not an appointed time to man upon earth? are not his days also like the days of an hireling?"
Job 7:1.

Our times on earth are appointed by God alone. No one knows how long you will live here. Only God knows. For some people, He might show them when their time comes to leave. Whether you know or not, you will keep that appointment one day.

"And as it is appointed unto men once to die, but after this the judgment."
Heb. 9:27.

"If a man die, shall he live again? all the days of my appointed time will I wait, till my change come."
Job 14:14.

There is an appointed time for every vision. No vision sees the light of day if it is not appointed by God. People have tried to accomplish things when it was not appointed by God and they have failed at it. However, when it is the God appointed time, it happens with much ease.

"For the vision is yet for an appointed time, but at the end it shall speak, and not lie: though it tarry, wait for it; because it will surely come, it will not tarry."
Hab. 2:3.

There is the **accepted time** which is as the occasion demands. This is spontaneous. The accepted time is the time God gives us to be saved, healed, delivered and blessed. This is when you take a decision to obey God, to accept His offers. You decide the accepted time because it depends on your decision to accept what God offers you.

"For he saith, I have heard thee in a time accepted, and in the day of salvation have I succoured thee: behold, now is the accepted time; behold, now is the day of salvation."
2 Cor. 6:2.

There is also the **convenient time** which is at ones leisure. This can be postponed. You have the capacity to make this time. You can choose to make it happen or not.

"As touching our brother Apollos, I greatly desired him to come unto you with the brethren: but his will was not at all to come at this time; but he will come when he shall have convenient time."
1 Cor. 16:12.

There is the **fullness of time** which is fixed. It is also spaced like the time a woman becomes pregnant and the time she delivers is spaced. It is normally nine months. This is also what we know as the proper time or the mature time. It cannot be fast tracked or speeded up. This is the time that takes its course. It is set by God alone.

"But when the fulness of the time was come, God sent forth his Son, made of a woman, made under the law."
Gal. 4:4.

There is also the **due time** which is distinct. It defers from person to person, place to place. What is due time for me may not be for you. For one person, due time can be twenty four hours time frame. While for another person, due time can be nine months. Not every child is born according to the fullness of time. Some babies are aborted just a few days from conception. Some are born six months from conception. We all have our due time to become saved, healed, delivered, blessed and fulfilled in life. While person succeeds at twenty, another succeeds at fifty or seventy. Never use your due time to judge others. Do not allow another person's due time pressure you to abort your dream or desire or destiny.

"And last of all he was seen of me also, as of one born out of due time."
1 Cor. 15:8.

It is important that you understand the times and seasons for you to work out the blessings of God in your life. When you understand the times and seasons, you will know what kind of work to do. You will know the kinds of word to work during your winter season so you can stay warm and live well. You will also know the kinds of work to do during your summer season so you don't die of heat. People have died prematurely because they were working in the wrong season of their lives.

"And of the children of Issachar, which were men that had understanding of the times, to know what Israel ought to do; the heads of them were two hundred; and all their brethren were at their commandment."
1 Chron. 12:32.

"So teach us to number our days, that we may apply our hearts unto wisdom.
Return, O Lord, how long? and let it repent thee concerning thy servants.
O satisfy us early with thy mercy; that we may rejoice and be glad all our days.
Make us glad according to the days wherein thou hast afflicted us, and the years wherein we have seen evil.
Let thy work appear unto thy servants, and thy glory unto their children.
And let the beauty of the Lord our God be upon us: and establish thou the work of our hands upon us; yea, the work of our hands establish thou it."
Psa. 90:12-17.

Purpose is another vital element of works. You can work because of the season and time, yet that may not be your purpose. Your purpose is your reason for being here. It is what you were designed for. Your purpose is that which brings out the attribute of God in you. Anything of God in you that is manifested is your true purpose for being here.

Anything you do that people seek to know who did it is where your purpose is. Anything you do is where you purpose is. Anything that exposes or exhibits you in the light of God's word is where your purpose is. Anything you do that makes you stand out of the crowd is your purpose for being here. Anything you do that makes you fit into the scheme of things is where your purpose is.

Any work you do according to God's purpose for your life will become a blessing to many. The work you did on earth will be a blessing passed on to your children. They will be the things for which you will be remembered when you are gone.

"Remember me, O my God, concerning this, and wipe not out my good deeds that I have done for the house of my God, and for the offices thereof."
Neh. 13:14.

What will you be remembered for? What good have you done to reserve a right, a portion and a memorial for yourself in God's kingdom now in this time and in the world to come?

What works will you do today, this week, this month, this year and the years to come that you will be remembered for years to come and beyond now? What good or service are you going to give or do that will be recorded in the book of remembrance for you? What offering or seed or donation will you give today that will become a memorial for you for good?

"Then answered I them, and said unto them, The God of heaven, he will prosper us; therefore we his servants will arise and build: but ye have no portion, nor right, nor memorial, in Jerusalem."
Neh. 2:20.

"And for the wood offering, at times appointed, and for the firstfruits. Remember me, O my God, for good."
Neh.13:31.

WEALTH

Wealth is one of the most powerful instruments of life. **Words are worked with wealth.** Wealth is made up of men, means and materials that strengthen us to work out our words. To match words with actions requires wealth. Jesus said, *"...for out of the abundance of the heart the mouth* *speaketh.* " Matt. 12:34. It is from the *abundance* or wealth of a man words are worked out or spoken.

This generation has a misplaced idea of what wealth really is. They have so far limited it to finances. Money. So we estimate people's wealth by how much money they have. Real wealth is determined by how much good you do. How much good things or good works that flow from you to people.

"[Charge them] to do good, to be rich in good works, to be liberal and generous of heart, ready to share [with others]. "
1 Tim. 6:18. (Amplified Version).

Your wealth is what you treasure. That which you value or place value on. The Greek word for **wealth** means that which is good for passing on to others. It is what you have that is good enough to be passed on to someone for his or her good. Anything you can pass on to someone that they can use to advance or advantage or add value to them is your wealth. Wealth must add value or advance or advantage you and anyone you give it to. If it will not add value to you or advance you or advantage you, certainly, it may not add value to another person. However, there are things you may have that will not add value to you until you give it to someone else. When you see it on someone else and you see how it makes them better or bigger, then you know that was your wealth. When you read or hear the report of what you gave or said or did, then you know that was your wealth.

You cannot **do** good or **give** good things if you are not good. It is out of what you **are** and **have** that you **can** give. There are people who try to do good but you just see that it is not real. It is a struggle for them. Good people give good things. Evil people give evil things. You cannot give good if you are evil. Even if what you are given is good, your evil DNA will reflect on your seeming good.

> *"Even so every good tree bringeth forth good fruit; but a*
> *corrupt tree bringeth forth evil fruit.*
> *A good tree cannot bring forth evil fruit, neither can a*
> *corrupt tree bring forth good fruit."*
> Matt. 7:17-18.

Most people who struggle to give, struggle because they don't have the grace to give. It takes grace to give. Grace is a divine influence upon the heart that reflects in the life. It is what makes a man liberal. This liberality Greek *charis* means to pleasure. You take delight in doing good. It gives you great pleasure.

> *"WE WANT to tell you further, brethren, about the grace*
> *(the favor and spiritual blessing) of God which has been*
> *evident in the churches of Macedonia [arousing in them the*
> *desire to give alms];*

*For in the midst of an ordeal of severe tribulation, their abundance of joy and their depth of poverty [together] have overflowed in wealth of lavish generosity on their part.
For, as I can bear witness, [they gave] according to their ability, yes, and beyond their ability; and [they did it] voluntarily,
Begging us most insistently for the favor and the fellowship of contributing in this ministration for [the relief and support of] the saints [in Jerusalem]."*
2 Cor. 8:1-4. Amplified Version.

Wealth is anything that is strength to you that you can pleasurably release to someone who is lacking or weak in that area.

"The rich man's wealth is his strong city: the destruction of the poor is their poverty."
Prov. 10:15.

The Greek word for **wealth** is also translated as resources. This is anything that is a source of supply or support. Anything you can use to generate support or supply is your wealth. *"...ye know that by this craft we have our wealth."* Acts 17:25.

Wealth is created by your craft, calling, career, charisma and character. With anyone or more of these you can create wealth anywhere and anytime. You can never be stranded.

Character has to do with a name. It could be your name or the name of someone. You can use somebody's name to create wealth. When I applied for my first visa at a European embassy, I was refused. However, I sent an email to the Billy Graham Evangelistic Association and they contacted the embassy to reverse the decision. Billy Graham's name opened up the door for me to Europe and Canada. Some people may not give you money. All you need from them is a recommendation with their name and that will open up great doors for you.

You can build your name to a point where your name can create wealth. If your name is good, you can also use it to create wealth. It takes time to build a name that can create wealth. There are people who have used my name to access certain persons for employment or opportunities they could never have gotten if not that they used my name. so I know that I am wealthy because my recommendation can open doors of business or ministry opportunities for some people. A good name is better than great riches.

"A good name is rather to be chosen than great riches, and loving favour rather than silver and gold."
Prov. 22:1.

Charisma is special ability or audacity or authority. It is divine ability when you are able to do something with ease that others struggle with. It is divine audacity when you word become the last order or door opener. It is divine authority when it is recognized and respected in places where this gives you priority or preferential treatment or recognition. It is divine enablement because it comes from God supernaturally. It is a gift of grace. This one comes from God. With it you can create wealth.

"But thou shalt remember the Lord thy God: for it is he that giveth thee power to get wealth, that he may establish his covenant which he sware unto thy fathers, as it is this day."
Deut.8:18.

Career is relative. It leans towards professional training. A course of training one pursues as a lifetime occupation. You can create wealth as a trained lawyer, medical doctor, pharmacist, accountant, engineer, actor, etc. Some of the wealthiest people in the world are professionals.

Calling is an opportunity or occasion that meets with someone and by seizing it they can create wealth. It may come in form of an appointment that exposes you to network with the right kind of people who have what you need to create wealth. My work as an evangelist is a calling. It is my response to God's call on my life to fulfill His great commission. When I am able to connect with the right people who are partners with me, I can create wealth with it. This is how great ministries have created wealth because they built a solid partnership base. Partnership is wealth base.

Craft is a trade or handwork. It is something you learn to do until you become skillful at it. It may not be your career or calling. With it you can create wealth.

"And through his policy also he shall cause craft to prosper in his hand..."
Dan. 8:25.

"Whom he called together with the workmen of like occupation, and said, Sirs, ye know that by this craft we have our wealth."
Acts 19:25.

Each one of us has been endowed with special abilities. It depends on you to discover and develop that ability so that you can deliver safely to your generation. By so doing you are doing good. You will be spreading your life into so many others.

Words, works and wealth have eternal consequences. They can form the traditions, customs, belief systems and religions of tomorrow's people. Besides, they can determine the eternal destination and dividends of each person. Consider this: the words you speak of Jesus today can determine your eternal destination. If you confess Him as Lord, then you are saved.

"For if you confess with your mouth that Jesus is Lord and believe in your heart that God raised him from the dead, you will be saved.
For it is by believing in your heart that you are made right with God, and it is by confessing with your mouth that you are saved."
Rom. 10:9,10. (New Living Translation)

If you confess Him before men, He will confess you before the Father in heaven. He cannot deny that He knows you on that day.

"Whosoever therefore shall confess me before men, him will I confess also before my Father which is in heaven.
But whosoever shall deny me before men, him will I also deny before my Father which is in heaven."
Matt. 10:32,33.

Your works can determine your eternal destination and rewards. You cannot earn salvation by works because it is free. It is by grace. Eph. 2:8-9. Rom. 3:20. Gal. 2:16. **We don't work to be saved but we must work out our salvation.** We must produce works or fruits that tell the world that we are saved. Matt.3:8. Rom.13:11-14. Phil. 2:12.

Our works shall be tried by fire to determine the quality of works done on earth. If your works survives the fire, then you are saved eternally with a reward from the Master. 1 Cor.3:12-15. We shall all be judged according to the **words** written in the books side by side our **works**. Our rewards shall be according to our works here on earth. Rev. 20:12-15.

Your wealth can also determine your eternal position. Some people could be very wealthy here on earth but are paupers in eternity. They are rich. They increase in goods. They have need for nothing. But they are wretched, poor and miserable eternally.

"Because thou sayest, I am rich, and increased with goods, and have need of nothing; and knowest not that thou art wretched, and miserable, and poor, and blind, and naked: I counsel thee to buy of me gold tried in the fire, that thou mayest be rich; and white raiment, that thou mayest be clothed, and that the shame of thy nakedness do not appear; and anoint thine eyes with eyesalve, that thou mayest see."
Rev. 3:17,18.

Wealth not stored down here but up there in heaven can determine your measure of influence in heaven.

"Lay not up for yourselves treasures upon earth, where moth and rust doth corrupt, and where thieves break through and steal:
But lay up for yourselves treasures in heaven, where neither moth nor rust doth corrupt, and where thieves do not break through nor steal:
For where your treasure is, there will your heart be also."
Matt. 6:19-21.

To store up wealth in heaven is to be rich in doing good, ready to distribute and willing to share.

"Charge them that are rich in this world, that they be not highminded, nor trust in uncertain riches, but in the living God, who giveth us richly all things to enjoy;
That they do good, that they be rich in good works, ready to distribute, willing to communicate;
Laying up in store for themselves a good foundation against the time to come, that they may lay hold on eternal life."
1 Tim 6:17-19.

3
THE SEEDS OF BLESSINGS

Seed is the connection between need and deed. Seed is a response to need. That response is the deed. The best response to a need is a seed. The seed carries the force of blessing. There is power in the seed.

NEED

The Hebrew word for **need** is the word *machcowr* that means to be deficient. It also means to be impoverished. It is rooted in the Hebrew word that means **to be without a necessity**, to be destitute, to lack, to fail and to be in want.

"If there is a poor man with you, one of your brothers, in any of your towns in your land which the LORD your God is giving you, you shall not harden your heart, nor close your hand from your poor brother;
But you shall freely open your hand to him, and shall generously lend him sufficient for his need in whatever he lacks."
Deut.15:7,8. (New American Standard Bible).

Every need demands satisfaction – that which is sufficient. If someone is in need of one hundred dollars and you give them part of it, the need has not been met. That is why the proverb that says that half bread is better than none is a great error. In fact, it is a grief to a hungry and desperate man. A bird in hand cannot be better than nine in the bush. Why do you think that the shepherd would leave ninety-nine sheep to look for just one that is missing? He could have been satisfied with the ninety-nine and careless about the missing one. But you see that missing one leaves a vacuum that the ninety-nine cannot fill. The need will always be there if it is not filled.

"And he spake this parable unto them, saying,
What man of you, having an hundred sheep, if he lose one
of them, doth not leave the ninety and nine in the
wilderness, and go after that which is lost, until he find it?
And when he hath found it, he layeth it on his shoulders,
rejoicing.
And when he cometh home, he calleth together his friends
and neighbours, saying unto them, Rejoice with me; for I
have found my sheep which was lost.
I say unto you, that likewise joy shall be in heaven over one
sinner that repenteth, more than over ninety and nine just
persons, which need no repentance."
Luke 15:3-7.

The cry of every need is not just enough but more than enough. Don't match the need. Give more than the need. God has shown us this by revealing Himself as the ***El-Shaddai*** – the One Who Is More Than Enough. He gives more than we need, pressed down, shaking together and running over.

"Give, and it shall be given unto you; good measure, pressed down, and shaken together, and running over, shall men give into your bosom. For with the same measure that ye mete withal it shall be measured to you again."
Luke 6:38.

Jesus also taught us to give more than the need.

"But I say unto you, That ye resist not evil: but whosoever shall smite thee on thy right cheek, turn to him the other also.
And if any man will sue thee at the law, and take away thy coat, let him have thy cloke also.
And whosoever shall compel thee to go a mile, go with him twain.
Give to him that asketh thee, and from him that would borrow of thee turn not thou away."
Matt. 5:39-42.

To withhold that which meets the need when you have it is a curse to you. God has vowed to fight those who hoard and hold back that which is designed to meet the needs of His work and workers here on earth. If God decides to fight you, you are finished.

"Withhold not good from them to whom it is due, when it is in the power of thine hand to do it.
Say not unto thy neighbour, Go, and come again, and to morrow I will give; when thou hast it by thee."
Prov. 3:27, 28.

"He that withholdeth corn, the people shall curse him: but blessing shall be upon the head of him that selleth it."
Prov. 11:26.

"Thus hath the Lord God shewed unto me: and behold a basket of summer fruit.
And he said, Amos, what seest thou? And I said, A basket of summer fruit. Then said the Lord unto me, The end is come upon my people of Israel; I will not again pass by them any more.
And the songs of the temple shall be howlings in that day, saith the Lord God: there shall be many dead bodies in every place; they shall cast them forth with silence.

Hear this, O ye that swallow up the needy, even to make the poor of the land to fail,
Saying, When will the new moon be gone, that we may sell corn? and the sabbath, that we may set forth wheat, making the ephah small, and the shekel great, and falsifying the balances by deceit?
That we may buy the poor for silver, and the needy for a pair of shoes; yea, and sell the refuse of the wheat?
The Lord hath sworn by the excellency of Jacob, Surely I will never forget any of their works.
Shall not the land tremble for this, and every one mourn that dwelleth therein? and it shall rise up wholly as a flood; and it shall be cast out and drowned, as by the flood of Egypt.
And it shall come to pass in that day, saith the Lord God, that I will cause the sun to go down at noon, and I will darken the earth in the clear day:
And I will turn your feasts into mourning, and all your songs into lamentation; and I will bring up sackcloth upon all loins, and baldness upon every head; and I will make it as the mourning of an only son, and the end thereof as a bitter day."
Amos 8:1-10.

We shall begin to see the judgment come on those who withhold that which is supposed to meet the need of God's work and workers. It happened to Ananias and Sapphira when they kept back some of the proceeds of their sold property from the apostles. Indeed they thought it was the apostles they were dealing with. Unknown to them, it was the Holy Ghost. You cannot lie against the Holy Ghost and get away, they died.

"But a certain man named Ananias, with Sapphira his wife, sold a possession,
And kept back part of the price, his wife also being privy to it, and brought a certain part, and laid it at the apostles' feet.
But Peter said, Ananias, why hath Satan filled thine heart to lie to the Holy Ghost, and to keep back part of the price of the land?
Whiles it remained, was it not thine own? and after it was sold, was it not in thine own power? why hast thou conceived this thing in thine heart? thou hast not lied unto men, but unto God.
And Ananias hearing these words fell down, and gave up the ghost: and great fear came on all them that heard these things.
And the young men arose, wound him up, and carried him out, and buried him.
And it was about the space of three hours after, when his wife, not knowing what was done, came in.
And Peter answered unto her, Tell me whether ye sold the land for so much? And she said, Yea, for so much.
Then Peter said unto her, How is it that ye have agreed together to tempt the Spirit of the Lord? behold, the feet of

*them which have buried thy husband are at the door, and
shall carry thee out.
Then fell she down straightway at his feet, and yielded up
the ghost: and the young men came in, and found her dead,
and, carrying her forth, buried her by her husband.
And great fear came upon all the church, and upon as many
as heard these things."*
Acts 5:1-11.

Many will be cast into outer darkness because they refuse to
meet the needs of God's work and workers.

When you shut your bowels of compassion to meet the needs
of the least or smallest of God's workers, you are not doing it
to them. It is the Lord Himself. On that day you will get your
report sheet.

*"Then shall the King say unto them on his right hand,
Come, ye blessed of my Father, inherit the kingdom
prepared for you from the foundation of the world:
For I was an hungred, and ye gave me meat: I was thirsty,
and ye gave me drink: I was a stranger, and ye took me in:
Naked, and ye clothed me: I was sick, and ye visited me: I
was in prison, and ye came unto me.*

Then shall the righteous answer him, saying, Lord, when saw we thee an hungred, and fed thee? or thirsty, and gave thee drink?
When saw we thee a stranger, and took thee in? or naked, and clothed thee?
Or when saw we thee sick, or in prison, and came unto thee?
And the King shall answer and say unto them, Verily I say unto you, Inasmuch as ye have done it unto one of the least of these my brethren, ye have done it unto me.
Then shall he say also unto them on the left hand, Depart from me, ye cursed, into everlasting fire, prepared for the devil and his angels:
For I was an hungred, and ye gave me no meat: I was thirsty, and ye gave me no drink:
I was a stranger, and ye took me not in: naked, and ye clothed me not: sick, and in prison, and ye visited me not.
Then shall they also answer him, saying, Lord, when saw we thee an hungred, or athirst, or a stranger, or naked, or sick, or in prison, and did not minister unto thee?
Then shall he answer them, saying, Verily I say unto you, Inasmuch as ye did it not to one of the least of these, ye did it not to me.
And these shall go away into everlasting punishment: but the righteous into life eternal."
Matt. 25:34-46.

I must be quick to state here that it is not everyone who comes with a need you have been designed to meet. You must be sensitive to the leanings of your heart. More importantly, **your seed will determine the need.** If there is no seed, you have no connection with that need.

SEED

The seed is more important than the need. The seed, Hebrew *zara* means that which has fruit in it. It must have the ability to produce fruit for the planter. It must be a fruit to the one receiving it whereas it is a seed to the planter. The Greek, *sperma* means an offspring or issue. It means an extender. It also means that which is kept for a sacrifice or that which is meant to be spread out or scattered.

Your seed must have the ability to produce fruits for you. There must be fruit in it. The only way to release that fruit is to plant the seed. When planted, it becomes an extension of you. It carries your life. It carries your blood. This is so because it issues out of you. It flows from you. It springs out of you.

You cannot afford to hold back your seed because it is your sacrifice. You are under duress, if I may borrow that word, to scatter it. In fact, it is a mandate. It is something you cannot eat. If you eat it, it will purge you. Just like the yam head. You cannot eat it because it is poisonous. It is meant to be planted. That is the earth's portion. The moment you release it to the earth, the earth will begin a process of returning it back to you with a fruit that can feed you and others for many days.

So, you are under compulsion to plant it. This you must do.

Jesus said, *"I must work the works of him that sent me, while it is day: the night cometh, when no man can work."* John 9:4.

DEED

The deed is the actual act of releasing your seed to meet a need. There are basically three levels of deed where your seed is. The first level is **sacrifice.** Every seed is a sacrifice because life is in it. There is blood in it. Life is in the blood. Gen. 9:4. The life is in the seed. The seed is the word. Luke 8:11. John 1:1,4. Each time a seed leaves the hand of the sower into the soil, that is a sacrifice. The sower could have eaten the seed. But by self-dinial, he plants the seed.

"Verily, verily, I say unto you, Except a corn of wheat fall into the ground and die, it abideth alone: but if it die, it bringeth forth much fruit."
John 12:24.

The next level of deed is **submission.** This is the act of putting yourself under the orders and instructions of someone. It is being obedient to instructions. **Obedience is higher than sacrifice.** It is better to obey than to sacrifice.

"And Samuel said, Hath the Lord as great delight in burnt offerings and sacrifices, as in obeying the voice of the Lord? Behold, to obey is better than sacrifice, and to hearken than the fat of rams."
1 Sam. 15:22.

"Sacrifice and offering thou didst not desire; mine ears hast thou opened: burnt offering and sin offering hast thou not required.
Then said I, Lo, I come: in the volume of the book it is written of me,
I delight to do thy will, O my God: yea, thy law is within my heart."
Psa. 40:6-8.

So, you don't go about scattering your seeds because you have to spread or sacrifice. The question is, by what order are you sowing the seed? Who told you to do what you are doing?

If you yield to God, you will become an instrument of obedience in His hands to accomplish His good pleasure. Get your orders from the Master. Mary said. ***"…Whatever He says to you, do it."*** John 2:5. (Amplified Version).

Jesus came as a sacrificial lamb. But He did not just give Himself as a sacrifice. He submitted Himself to the orders and instructions of His Father. He was obedient to the death of the cross.

"And being found in fashion as a man, he humbled himself, and became obedient unto death, even the death of the cross."
Phil. 2:8.

"Though he were a Son, yet learned he obedience by the things which he suffered."
Heb. 5:8.

Whatever you do, if you do it as to the Lord in obedience to His word then you have gone beyond sacrifice. Be rest assured that there shall be a reward from the Lord to you. He is a rewarder. He will reward your deeds of obedience. Col. 3:23. Heb. 11:6.

The third level of deed is **service**. This is the highest because this is where God created man to live: to serve God totally eternally. To serve, Hebrew *abad* means to work, to wrought and to worship.

Man was created to worship God. To worship, Hebrew *shachah* means to prostrate, bow down, fall down flat and to stoop. Man was created upright but He must bow down before God in worship.

"Thou art worthy, O Lord, to receive glory and honour and power: for thou hast created all things, and for thy pleasure they are and were created."
Rev. 4:11.

God is seeking for worshippers. He is looking for those who will worship Him with their whole being - spirit, soul and body – prostrate before Him. And, it must be real.

"But the hour cometh, and now is, when the true worshippers shall worship the Father in spirit and in truth: for the Father seeketh such to worship him. God is a Spirit: and they that worship him must worship him in spirit and in truth."
John 4:23-24.

Man was created to wrought or accomplish God's purpose. Every designer has a purpose for their products. God, the Master Designer, has a purpose for each one of His creation including you. Apart from worship to God, you need to accomplish His specific purpose for your life. The reason why Jehovah God guides His word with jealousy is because He wants to ensure that the purpose tied to that word is accomplished. You are God's word sent to planet earth on assignment. You must fulfill it.

"So shall my word be that goeth forth out of my mouth: it shall not return unto me void, but it shall accomplish that which I please, and it shall prosper in the thing whereto I sent it."
Isa 55:11.

Man was created to work. The word **work** Hebrew **melakah** means ministry or business. It connotes the idea of someone who is deputizing for a superior or in the employment of someone. The manner of doing the work is what is emphasized here. Is the work done with dispatch*? "...the king's business required haste."* 1 Sam. 21:8.

*"Let a man so account of us, as of the ministers of Christ, and stewards of the mysteries of God.
Moreover it is required in stewards, that a man be found faithful."*
1 Cor. 4:1-2.

In planting your seeds, do it with speed. Be quick in obeying God so you don't lose the energy that the order or instruction carries. Do it faithfully. Do it with fervent zeal.

"Not slothful in business; fervent in spirit; serving the Lord."
Rom. 12:11.

Do it bountifully and cheerfully.

"Therefore I thought it necessary to exhort the brethren, that they would go before unto you, and make up beforehand your bounty, whereof ye had notice before, that

the same might be ready, as a matter of bounty, and not as of covetousness.
But this I say, He which soweth sparingly shall reap also sparingly; and he which soweth bountifully shall reap also bountifully.
Every man according as he purposeth in his heart, so let him give; not grudgingly, or of necessity: for God loveth a cheerful giver."
2 Cor. 9:5-7.

Do it because you will be richly rewarded and that on time.

"And let us not be weary in well doing: for in due season we shall reap, if we faint not.
As we have therefore opportunity, let us do good unto all men, especially unto them who are of the household of faith."
Gal. 6:9-10.

4

MY TESTIMONY

When I finished writing the third chapter of this book, I felt a nudge in my spirit to add one more chapter. I asked the Lord, what should I title it? That was how this chapter came to be: My Testimony.

"The Revelation of Jesus Christ, which God gave unto him, to shew unto his servants things which must shortly come to pass; and he sent and signified it by his angel unto his servant John:
Who bare record of the word of God, and of the testimony of Jesus Christ, and of all things that he saw.
Blessed is he that readeth, and they that hear the words of this prophecy, and keep those things which are written therein: for the time is at hand."
Rev. 1:1-3.

Testimony is very powerful and instrumental in making the devil crumble before us. It is a weapon for warfare. It can make winning easy. Testimony is like a profile or curriculum vitae or resume. A good testimony can open up great doors. A great testimony can send chills on your opponents. One testimony can provoke several others.

"And they overcame him by the blood of the Lamb, and by the word of their testimony; and they loved not their lives unto the death."
Rev. 12:11.

In the Old Testament, the ark of God's presence was called the **Testimony**.

"As the Lord commanded Moses, so Aaron laid it up before the Testimony, to be kept."
Ex. 16:34.

There were three things in the Testimony namely, the rod of Aaron that budded, the bread from heaven called manna and the tablets that the Ten Commandments were written.

"Which had the golden censer, and the ark of the covenant overlaid round about with gold, wherein was the golden pot that had manna, and Aaron's rod that budded, and the tables of the covenant."
Heb. 9:4.

In the New Testament, we see the Testimony as the Spirit of Jesus. The testimony of Jesus is the spirit of prophecy that comes on us to dwell with us.

*"Who bare record of the word of God, and of the testimony of Jesus Christ, and of all things that he saw.
I John, who also am your brother, and companion in tribulation, and in the kingdom and patience of Jesus Christ, was in the isle that is called Patmos, for the word of God, and for the testimony of Jesus Christ."*
Rev. 1:2,9.

"And the dragon was wroth with the woman, and went to make war with the remnant of her seed, which keep the commandments of God, and have the testimony of Jesus Christ."
Rev. 12:17.

"And I fell at his feet to worship him. And he said unto me, See thou do it not: I am thy fellowservant, and of thy brethren that have the testimony of Jesus: worship God: for the testimony of Jesus is the spirit of prophecy."
Rev. 19:10.

Each time we stand to testify of Jesus, the Spirit of prophecy is at work. That Spirit will cause your rod, no matter how lifeless it is, to blossom. The same Spirit shall cause supernatural provisions to come to you. The same Spirit shall cause you to walk in God's word.

"But if the Spirit of him that raised up Jesus from the dead dwell in you, he that raised up Christ from the dead shall also quicken your mortal bodies by his Spirit that dwelleth in you."
Rom. 8:11.

Testimony is a personal record or report of what happened. It is a witness. It is evidence. It is the down payment or proof producer.

"And you also became God's people when you heard the true message, the Good News that brought you salvation. You believed in Christ, and God put his stamp of ownership on you by giving you the Holy Spirit he had promised. The Spirit is the guarantee that we shall receive what God has promised his people, and this assures us that God will give complete freedom to those who are his. Let us praise his glory!"
Eph. 1:13-14. Today's English Version.

The law requires that a man must testify before the priest after a healing miracle.

"And Jesus saith unto him, See thou tell no man; but go thy way, shew thyself to the priest, and offer the gift that Moses commanded, for a testimony unto them."
Matt. 8:4.

Early in ministry as an itinerant evangelist, I had a gospel crusade somewhere. All I needed then was about ten thousand naira only. That was twenty nine years ago. I still remember how I called on several friends and partners to plant a seed towards that harvest. Some of my friends and partners could have met that need. But they missed the opportunity by passing it by just like the priest and Levite Jesus talked about below.

"And Jesus answering said, A certain man went down from Jerusalem to Jericho, and fell among thieves, which stripped him of his raiment, and wounded him, and departed, leaving him half dead.
And by chance there came down a certain priest that way: and when he saw him, he passed by on the other side.
And likewise a Levite, when he was at the place, came and looked on him, and passed by on the other side.

But a certain Samaritan, as he journeyed, came where he was: and when he saw him, he had compassion on him, And went to him, and bound up his wounds, pouring in oil and wine, and set him on his own beast, and brought him to an inn, and took care of him. And on the morrow when he departed, he took out two pence, and gave them to the host, and said unto him, Take care of him; and whatsoever thou spendest more, when I come again, I will repay thee. Which now of these three, thinkest thou, was neighbour unto him that fell among the thieves?"
Luke 10:30-36.

We had the crusade to the glory of God. It was a struggle but we conquered. A few weeks later, there was a tragedy in the city. This badly affected a couple of my friends. One of them had invested the sum of ten thousand naira in an investment house that was notorious for almost doubling the money after one month. This precious partner heard the call to invest into God's business and turned deaf ear.

A couple of weeks later the investment house was taken over by the then military government because it was illegal. All those who invested their hard earned money including a couple of my dear friends and partners lost all. They heard the call to invest into the treasury that moth and rust cannot corrupt. Their response was a deaf ear.

I will never forget a church I had a weekend revival with. The presence of God was awesome. Towards the end of the meeting, the Holy Ghost directed me to tell the pastor to lead his members and the entire church to plant a seed into my ministry. The pastor testified to the fact that God spoke to his heart too. But he chose to postpone it. Till today, he never did.

Some months after this meeting, a spiritual wind blew the church. It was so bad that the church scattered. The church is still trying to keep afloat after so many years.

When God instructs, act with speed. I had a meeting with one of my dear friend. After my ministry of the word under a strong prophetic unction, the pastor came up and said that the Lord impressed it on his heart to sow his car to the church. As a church, they planted that car seed into my life. That was a sacrifice. But it was more than a sacrifice because it was in obedience to God's order.

After my friend planted this seed, his miracles began to unfold. His company manager sent him a memo eleven days later to get ready to travel to Korea. That trip alone made him richer financially to the extent that he loaned his church half a million naira for a major event after making his own sacrifice. Later, his company withdrew the small official car he was using and gave him three brand new four-wheel drive.

The church was not left out. A few days later, a man he never knew walked up to him and told him that he would sponsor his ministry on television. This man single handedly paid for the television broadcast for several years. He has even promised to do more than that. While I was in the United States, he sent me an e-mail of the blessings that were still coming in as a result of that seed. Today, the church is exploding in growth. Someone bought a bus and a generator. The testimonies are still pouring in because this my friend obeyed God.

I want to turn the table toward you right now. *"This will be a time (an opportunity) for you to bear testimony."* Luke 21:13. (Amplified Version).

There is a seed in your hand that you must release for your miracles to begin to turn in. Don't say, **'I don't have anything…'** That which you have, release it to God today in obedience to the Spirit of prophesy that has come on you by reading the prophetic words in this book. As you obey, I pray for a confirmation of God's word in your experience in Jesus name. Amen!

WHY I CHOSE JESUS CHRIST?

Someone asked me many years ago, Mike, why did you accept Jesus Christ? I could have become an atheist, a Muslim, etc. Why Jesus Christ?

My answer to that question is for basically three reasons and the fourth one will blow your mind.

One, I accepted Jesus Christ because I needed a Father. A father is a life source. That means you came from him. According to the law of sustenance, you can only be sustained by your source. Fish came out of water and thus can only be sustained in a water environment. If you put it on land, no matter how nice looking, it will die in no distant time. I realized that God is my Source. I can only be sustained by Him. I discovered that I couldn't have a personal relationship with Him through any other one or way except through Jesus Christ. John 14:6. Acts 4:12.

Like a fish out of water in a land environment, you and I continue to struggle to survive until we reconnect with our natural habitat or source. This is God your Father. This happens only through Jesus Christ. You will never be fulfilled or become eternally relevant until you accept Jesus Christ into your heart as your personal Lord and Master. Then will you be able to connect with God your Source. Then will you know what it means to be sustained by the grace of God.

Two, I accepted Jesus Christ because I needed a friend. Man was designed to relate with his environment and people. Nobody can survive as an island. You will need friends in your life. For me, it is very easy to make friends. As I grew up, my life became messed up by the friends I had. Friends betrayed me. Some battered me. Yet some others left me each time after our relationship with bruises. The marks will always be there. It was my search unknown to me for the real friend that got me into such relationships. I did not know about the Friend that sticks closer than a brother. Proverbs 18:24.

Friends have scorned me like they did Job. Job's friends turned aside from him (Job 6:18). They laughed him to scorn (Job 12:4). He was such a laughing stock that his eyes poured out tears to God (Job 16:20). His kinfolks failed him. His friends forgot him (Job 19:14). I have been there.

I needed a friend who will love me the way I am. I found this Friend in Jesus. He is God who became Abraham's Friend (Gen. 18:17. 2 Chron. 20:7). What a Friend He was to Abraham that even when Abraham lied about his wife, God rebuked the king to restore Abraham's wife (Gen. 12:10-20. 20:1-18.). A true friend will be there for you in good times and bad ones. Jesus is the best Friend I have ever had in my life (John 15:14).

You will never know a true friend outside of Jesus Christ. Your parents? Spouse? Relatives? Classmates? Colleagues? I choose Jesus Christ because He will be there for me all the time. He said so and I believe Him.

Three, I needed a future. Life is past, present and future. I have seen the past, it was both good and bad. I cannot do anything about it. It is gone forever. I failed in the past. I did all the bad things in the past. But it is gone leaving me with the consequences of my wrong choices and deeds. Now I am in the present. What can I do to make the difference for my future? This is what I am concerned with today. I discovered that it is only in Jesus Christ that His precious blood washes my past away. My today is secured with His ever-abiding presence because He is a very present help. My tomorrow is taken care of because He told me not to worry about it.

I have a beautiful future in Jesus Christ because of what He did for me at the cross. I sinned and deserved to die. He took my sins and died in my place. In exchange, He gave me His very life, abundant life.

The fourth reason is that He changed my life. Religion tries to change people by principles, philosophies and practices. But Jesus came into my life without Him putting any demands on me to do things to earn His forgiveness. All He asked from me was to believe and receive Him. I did and found that my life is just changing every day. When I started this journey, I did not look like what I am today. I am not the same every day. I can assure you that by tomorrow I will become better. Until the day when I shall be changed permanently at the sound of the trump of God. From that point, I will put on immortality and incorruption. Sin shall never have dominion over me for all eternity. Is this not the kind of life you really desire from the deepest part of your being?

Today, my friend, you must make up your mind to receive Jesus Christ or reject Him. It is your choice. If you want to choose Jesus Christ, it is easy. Just say out loud:
Jesus, I believe you came to this world because You love me. Your love constrained You to the cross where You died for my sins to be forgiven me. Jesus, I believe. Come into my heart today. Wash me with Your precious blood. Make me a new person whose love and passion will be for You the rest of my life on earth. Jesus, You are the Lord of my life from this day forward. Thank You for saving me in Jesus name. Amen.

If you have prayed this prayer, do write me today and I will send you some materials to help you in this journey to become all that God has designed you to be.

PARTNER WITH US

When God gives one man a vision, it will require the participation of several others to fulfill that vision. No single individual can carry out God's vision because God gives according to His size. Anyone who tries to fulfill God's vision by themselves either will get frustrated or finished off. In 1989, God told Brother Mike, *'Son, take this gospel and miracle power of the living Christ to the nations – impacting lives and destinies with the WORD.'* Since then, that word has been the driving force to reaching 30 million souls in at least 50 nations.

"And they beckoned unto their partners, which were in the other ship, that they should come and help them. And they came, and filled both the ships, so that they began to sink." Luke 5:7.

Through this message, we are beckoning on you to come alongside with us through your support and partnership. Help us reach millions around the world. Help us to fill our boat with a massive harvest. The beauty of this partnership is that when you help us, our boat and your boat will be filled. Together, we shall have a net breaking and boat sinking harvest.

Three things you CAN do to help us:

1. You can PRAY. Zech. 10:1. Acts 4:28-30. Eph. 6:18-20. Your prayers travel faster than the speed of light. You can commit to pray for us on a regular basis.

2. You can PLANT your seed of any size. Your money or material seed is the mobile force that moves the gospel from person to person and place to place. Your money or material is YOU GOing places you may not have the chance to be physically. Give generously. You can give your offering and seeds with your credit or debit card with this email address: ***amamieye@yahoo.co.uk*** through ***https://www.pay.google.com*** or MAWO account details:

GTBank account number 0038894924. If you are outside Nigeria, you can give through MoneyGram.com for free. GTBank accepts money through MoneyGram for free. Use it while the opportunity last.

In Nigeria, you can give by using your bank code as follows:

For offering, dial: *bankcode*000*491+amount#

For tithes, dial: *bankcode*000*492+amount#

If you are using GTBank for instance, your bank code is 737, so you can dial: *737*000*491+amount#

If you are in the United States of America, you can give your offering to Bank of America account number 0905418443. ABA Routing number is: 121000358.
With Zelle, send to: **amamieye@yahoo.co.uk**

If you are in the United Kingdom, you can give your offering to NatWest Bank account number 52344819. Sort code 602112.

3. You can PARTICIPATE with us as you join forces with us in any location near you. I look forward to see you as we gather together a net breaking and boat sinking harvest. Luke 5:7. If you hear a voice saying, ignore this message, just know that it is the old serpent from the Garden. Tell that voice to shut up because you are the sheep of Jesus and you only obey the voice of your Master Jesus Christ. John 10:27. Thank you very much for obeying His voice in your heart and for being a part of what God is doing with us around the nations.

FOR MORE INFORMATION

Send in your testimonies to let us know how this devotional has been a blessing to you.

Send in your prayer requests as well.

Stand with us to help us reach thirty million souls in fifty nations.

For more spiritual help, counseling and prayer ministration, contact:

Bishop Michael O. Amamieye
Michael Amamieye Word Outreach, International
a/k/a Aggressive Faith Ministries
Plot 13 Walter Akpana Lay Out off 394 Ikwerre Road
Mile 5 Rumueprikom
P. O. Box 12378
Port Harcourt
Nigeria.

Hotlines: +2348050987377, +2349018006296
U.S.A: +19162456157
WhatsApp: +2348036732188
www.aggressivefaith.org
E-mail: info@aggressivefaith.org

ABOUT THE AUTHOR

Psalm 40:2,3 is a keynote to the life and ministry of Michael O. Amamieye. He was radically saved, healed and delivered from the power of darkness that endangered his youth. He is a living proof of God's matchless and abundant grace.

Since 1983, Brother Mike has been president, pastor and pioneer of several fellowships, churches and movements. He is instrumental in birthing many sons and daughters unto glory. He is a consecrated bishop with an oversight that reaches five continents.

In 1984, the Lord called Brother Mike to world evangelism with a mandate to *take the gospel and miracle power of the risen Christ to the nations – impacting lives and destinies with the WORD!* He is the President of **Michael Amamieye Word Outreach International** *also known as* **Aggressive Faith Ministries** with headquarters in the Garden City of Port Harcourt, Nigeria. Through this ministry, Brother Mike has a mandate to win at least thirty million souls in at least fifty nations to Christ with the simple proclamation of the gospel of Christ with evidence that brings salvation, healing, deliverance, blessing and joy.

An evangelist by calling, he is a graduate of the Billy Graham School of Evangelism. A member of Proclamation Evangelism Network, an associate evangelist with the Next

Generation Alliance and Global Network of Evangelists founded by the Luis Palau Association. He has been interviewed on Decision Today Radio broadcast and Decision magazine both of which are owned by the Billy Graham Evangelistic Association.

In 2003, Brother Mike was given the key to the City of East Cleveland, Ohio by the Mayor in a public ceremony. In 2012, LEADS Africa recognized him with the prestigious award as an icon of nation building for his contribution to the nation. In 2014, The Voice Magazine in the Netherlands honored him with the Spiritual Leadership award for his spiritual leadership. In 2019, he was conferred with a honorary degree of Doctor of Ministry by Triune Biblical University Global Extension, USA. He is a member of the senate of the Christian Judicial Institute, Nigeria. He is a member of the board of Fields of Glory International, USA.

Brother Mike has taken the gospel to at least seventy two countries so far. He is on high demand in crusades, conferences and conventions around the world.

He is the author of more than twenty books. He is a prolific and thought captivating writer with many of his works published in newsletters, magazines and newspapers around the world.

Bishop Mike is happily married to Princess Monivi, an ordained minister of the gospel and a health practitioner.

They are blessed with two children, Edwina Aleme and Mehetabel Favour.

Welcome To The Partner Family

"They signaled to their partners in other boat to come and take hold with them. And they came and filled both the boats, so that they began to sink." Luke 5:7. (Amplified Version).

Since the Lord gave me the vision of a massive harvest of souls through the mandate to reach 30 million souls for whom Christ died in at least 50 countries, I have not ceased to signal my partners *to come and take hold with me*.

Through our mass evangelistic crusades, we are seeing many become born again. It is amazing as God is giving us the gates of our enemies. We are seeing hardened criminals, cult leaders, gang leaders, etc, become born again.

This is possible because of the sacrifices of committed partners who have responded to our calls.

Now, it is your turn to respond to my signal. I want to give you an opportunity to fill your boat with miracles until it begins to sink.

Please check appropriate boxes:

☐ **I WANT TO BECOME A MONTHLY PARTNER.** I am expecting my partner information packet with more details. My offering is enclosed to start my partnership. I am willing to commit monthly: ☐ **$15** ☐ **$20** ☐ **$25** ☐ **$50** ☐ **$100**

☐ **I WANT TO HELP SPONSOR A CRUSADE.** Enclosed is my special one-time gift of: ☐ **$1000** ☐ **$2000** ☐ **$3000** ☐ **$**_________

Tear this form and send to us with your prayer requests. Use the address you find in this book.

www.ingramcontent.com/pod-product-compliance
Lightning Source LLC
Chambersburg PA
CBHW031353160726
47993CB00002B/949